AUTOMATED TESTING SERIES-1

ARCHITECTURE DESIGN INSTALLATION & SETUP AT A GLANCE

Abu Sayed Mahfuz

Automated Testing Series 1
Architecture & Design Installation Setup At a Glance
© 2024 by Abu Sayed Mahfuz,

International Standard Book Number:

This book contains information obtained from personal experiences and highly regarded sources. Reasonable efforts have been made to publish reliable data and information, but the author and publisher cannot assume responsibility for the validity of all materials or the consequences of their use.

Except as permitted under U.S. Copyright Law, no part of this book may be reprinted, reproduced, transmitted, or utilized in any form by any electronic, mechanical, or other means, now known or hereafter invented, including photocopying, microfilming, and recording, or in any information storage or retrieval system, without written permission from the author.

Names: Mahfuz, Abu Sayed, author. Title: Automated Testing Series: Architecture Design Installation Setup At a Glance
/ Author, Abu Sayed Mahfuz.

Copyright © 2024 Abu Sayed Mahfuz
All rights reserved.
ISBN: 9798333766083

Acknowledgments

First, to my departed parents whom were always inspiration and spirit for me. To extended family, to all my professors, specially Professor Dan Shoemaker, who taught me, inspired me and helped me whenever I needed any help. Who also have direct and indirect contribution on me writing this book.

Table of Contents

Acknowledgments iii
Preface 9
Install Java 11
    Check if Java is installed 11
    Java is not recognized before config 11
          Type jdk to Download 12
    Download Latest version 12
    Correct version for your OS 13
    Install JDK from Download folder 14
    Location where JDK to be installed 14
    Verify in cmd prompt 15
    Verify in Program files 16
    Java folder is configured 16
Variable settings 17
    Env Variable set up 17
    Environment Variables 18
    Add the JAVA_HOME 18
    Click on 'NEW' 19
        New System Variable module pops up 19
    Type Variable name-JAVA_HOME 20
    Go to the folder where Java located 20
          Copy the Path-Address 20
          Paste the copied path 21
          Click OK 21
    Edit PATH -Env Variable 22
          Select Path on Env. Variable Module then Click on Edit button 22
    Update the PATH variable 22
    Create new path Env variable Module 23
    Crate a Click on New Button 23
    Paste the bin folder Path here 24
    To find path Go to Bin folder in Java folder 24
    Copy the Bin folder path 25
    Paste java > bin address into the new line 25
    Click OK 26

v

Now Check if Java Installed 26
JAVA Recognized after env variable config 27
Echo %JAVA_HOME% 27
Verify Java Installation in Program 27
Verify Java & jdk inside Program file 28

Install Eclipse IDE 29

Download & Install Eclipse 30
Download correct and latest version 31
Eclipse IDE for Java Developer 31
User Agreement 32
Remember Location Eclipse to Installed 32

Start Java Project in Eclipse 33

CLICK ON FILE > NEW > JAVA PROJECT 33
Give a Project Name 34
PROJECT VIEW IN ECLIPSE 35
Update to latest version of Eclipse 36

Apache Maven 37

DOWNLOAD MAVEN 38
Download the correct version bin – zip file 38
Unzip- extract the folder 38

Maven Env Setup 39

Locate 'Maven Home' in your computer 39
Copy the Address 40
Paste in the 40
Edit Maven Path 41
Check if Maven installation displays 42

Start a Maven Project 43

Select the Maven Project 43
Convert Java Project to Maven Project 44
POM.XML file added to the project 45

Selenium 47

Selenium with different version/options 48
Ruby 48
C# 48
Java 48

vi

   Python 48
   JavaScirpt 48
 Add Selenium-Java 48
 SELENIUM DEPENDENCY FILE 49
   Add Dependency file to Dependencies in Pom.xml file.... 49
 Copy selenium Dependency 50
 Paste Dependency added in to POM file 50

TestNG 51

 TESTNG INSTALLATION & SETUP 52
   Go to mvnrepository.com and search for TestNG 52
   Click on TestNG and latest version and 52
   copy the code 52
   Paste in to your Project POM.xml file 53
 Added Selenium & TestNG Dependencies: 53

Junit 55

 JUNIT INSTALLATION AND SETUP 56
 SAMPLE DEPENDENCIES 57

Preface

Software Quality Assurance is one of the most demanding Job fields. Like anyone in Information Technology, I have noticed and realize the important and necessity of Quality and Security in my experience in Information Technology for 17 years.

During my Masters degree classes in Computer Information Systems in 2005, my concentrated study was on QA and Information Security, I have thoroughly studied IEEE and ISO Standards specially ISO/IEC 9126, ISO-15408, ISO-17799, COBIT & OCTAVE.
In my first book for IT Professionals "Software Quality Assurance Integrating Testing Security and Audit", I have thoroughly discussed and evaluated the Security and Quality Standards.
As time has evolved, our reading habit has also changed, especially IT professionals. Based on the Circumstances, I have decided to produce books precise, visual, focused and bullet point based.
I assure; you don't have to read a lot. You can just glance through, go to the point.

The advocacy of this book is the more visual and practical, and step by step. Items in this book can be used for Power Point presentation, in notepad or even on your visual board. This book is not mean to be descriptive, its mostly focused and point based. If you know and understand key words I have use, you will be good to go.

Install Java

Check if Java is installed

Java --version
Java is not recognized before Installation and configuration

```
C:\Users\mahfuz>java --version
'java' is not recognized as an internal or external command,
operable program or batch file.

C:\Users\mahfuz>java -v
'java' is not recognized as an internal or external command,
operable program or batch file.

C:\Users\mahfuz>java --v
'java' is not recognized as an internal or external command,
operable program or batch file.

C:\Users\mahfuz>
```

Java is not recognized before config

```
C:\Users\mahfuz>java --version
'java' is not recognized as an internal or external command,
operable program or batch file.

C:\Users\mahfuz>java -v
'java' is not recognized as an internal or external command,
operable program or batch file.

C:\Users\mahfuz>java --v
'java' is not recognized as an internal or external command,
operable program or batch file.

C:\Users\mahfuz>
```

Type jdk to Download

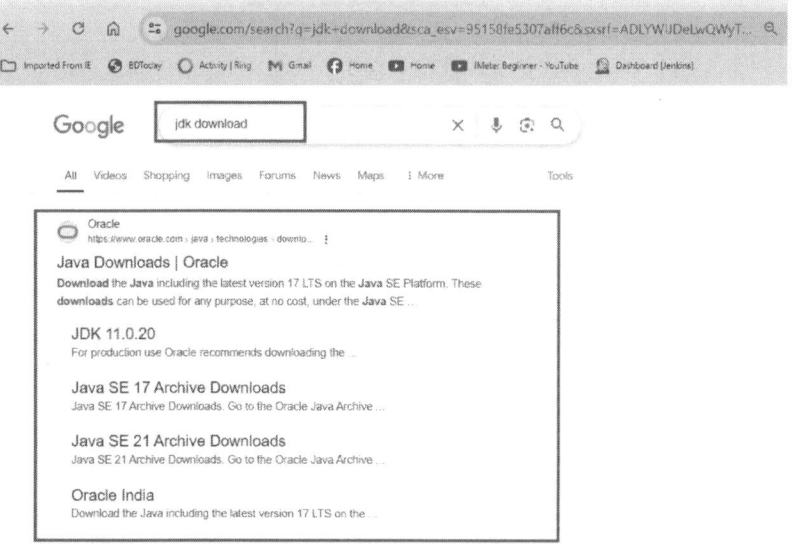

Download Latest version

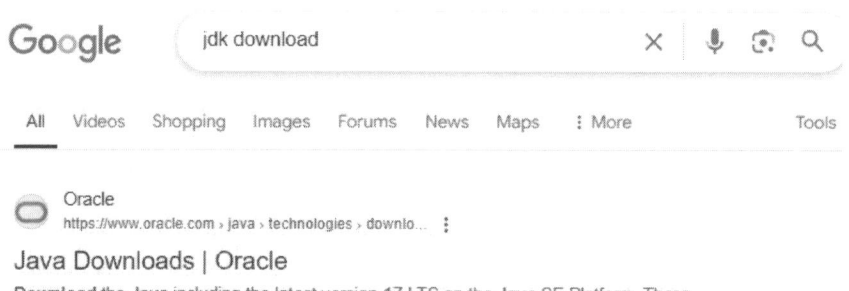

Correct version for your OS

Download Correct version for Windows or Mac as you need
Applicable link for applicable OS

JDK Development Kit 22.0.2 downloads

JDK 22 binaries are free to use in production and free to redistribute, at no cost, under the Oracle No-Fee Terms and Conditions (NFTC).

JDK 22 will receive updates under these terms, until September 2024, when it will be superseded by JDK 23.

Linux   macOS   **Windows**

Product/file description	File size	Download
x64 Compressed Archive	184.16 MB	https://download.oracle.com/java/22/latest/jdk-22_windows-x64_bin.zip (sha256)
x64 Installer	164.35 MB	https://download.oracle.com/java/22/latest/jdk-22_windows-x64_bin.exe (sha256)
x64 MSI Installer	163.09 MB	https://download.oracle.com/java/22/latest/jdk-22_windows-x64_bin.msi (sha256)

Being Downloaded

Linux x64 RPM Package	155.75 MB	https://download.oracle.com/java/18/archive/jdk-18.0.2
macOS Arm 64 Compressed Archive	168.42 MB	https://download.oracle.com/java/18/archive/jdk-18.0.2
macOS 64 DMG Installer	167.81 MB	https://download.oracle.com/java/18/archive/jdk-18.0.2
macOS x64 Compressed Archive	170.48 MB	https://download.oracle.com/java/18/archive/jdk-18.0.2
macOS x64 DMG Installer	169.88 MB	https://download.oracle.com/java/18/archive/jdk-18.0.2
Windows x64 Compressed Archive	172.79 MB	https://download.oracle.com/java/18/archive/jdk-18.0.2
Windows x64 Installer	153.37 MB	https://download.oracle.com/java/18/archive/jdk-18.0.2
Windows x64 msi Installer	152.25 MB	https://download.oracle.com/java/18/archive/jdk-18.0.2

https://download.oracle.com/java/18/archive/jdk-18.0.2_windows-x64_bin.exe

jdk-18.0.2_window...exe
28.3/153 MB, 6 secs left

Install JDK from Download folder

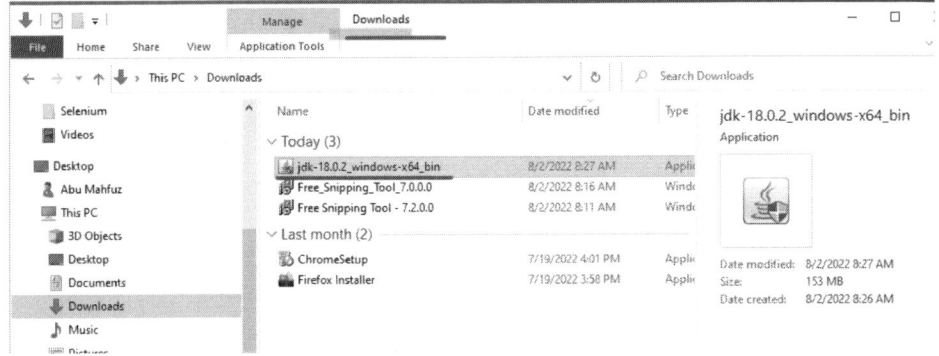

Location where JDK to be installed

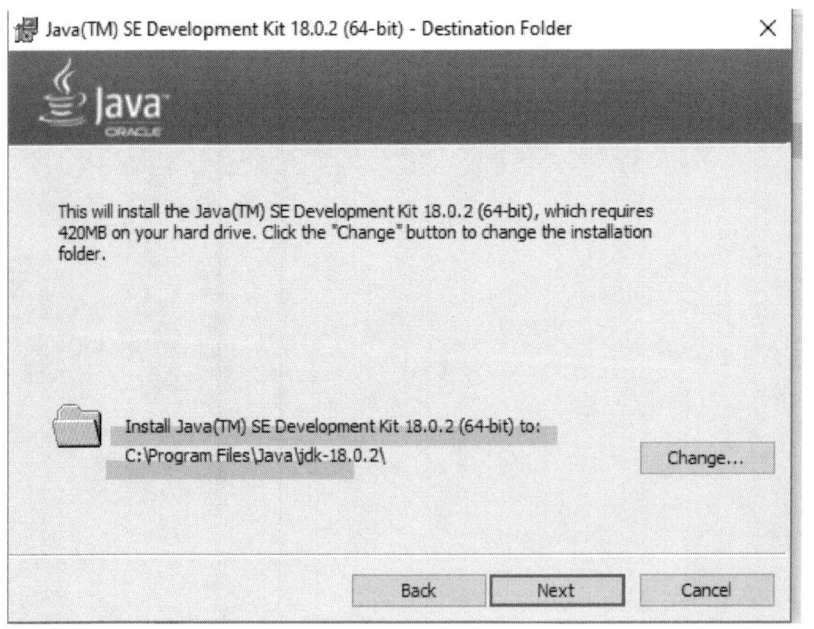

Successfully installed

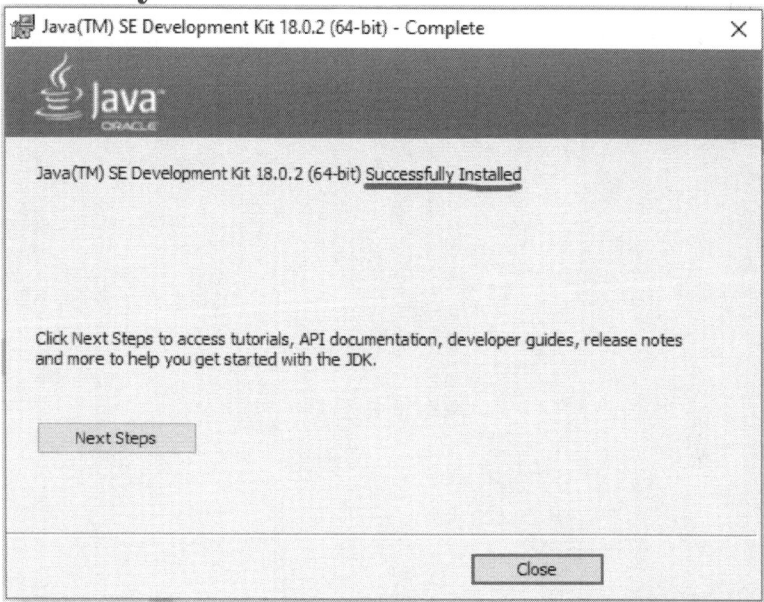

Verify in cmd prompt

```
C:\Users\mahfu>java --version
java 19 2022-09-20
Java(TM) SE Runtime Environment (build 19+36-2238)
Java HotSpot(TM) 64-Bit Server VM (build 19+36-2238, mixed mode, sharing)

C:\Users\mahfu>
```

Verify in Program files

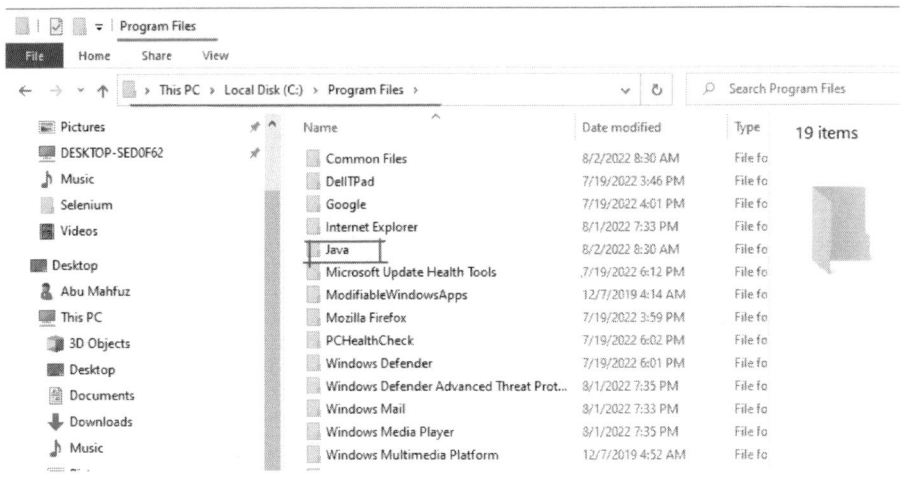

Java folder is configured

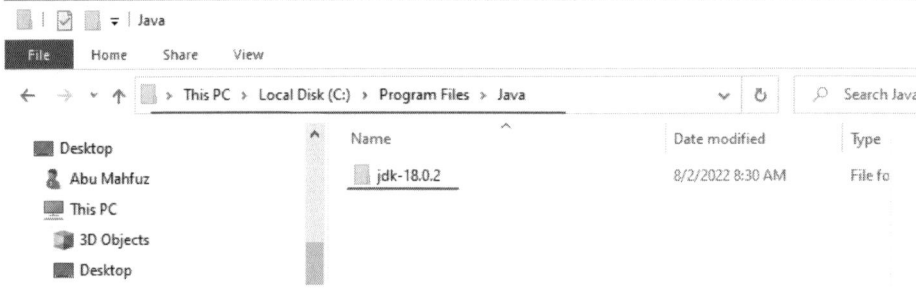

Variable settings

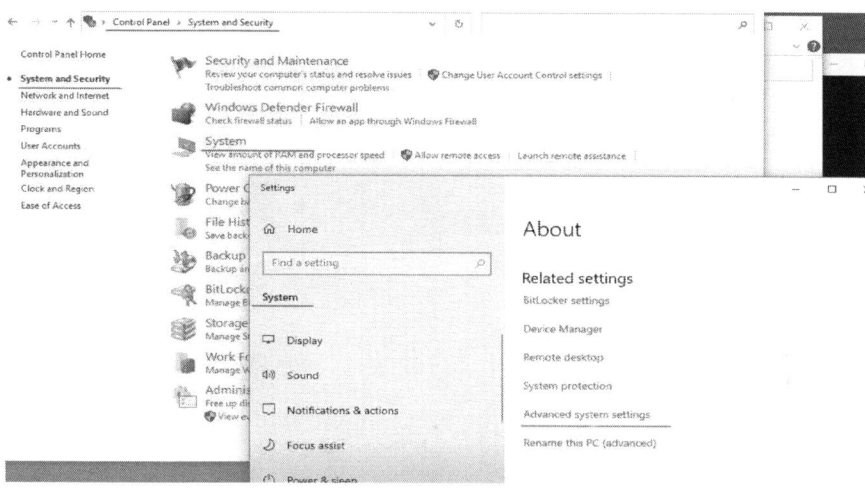

Env Variable set up

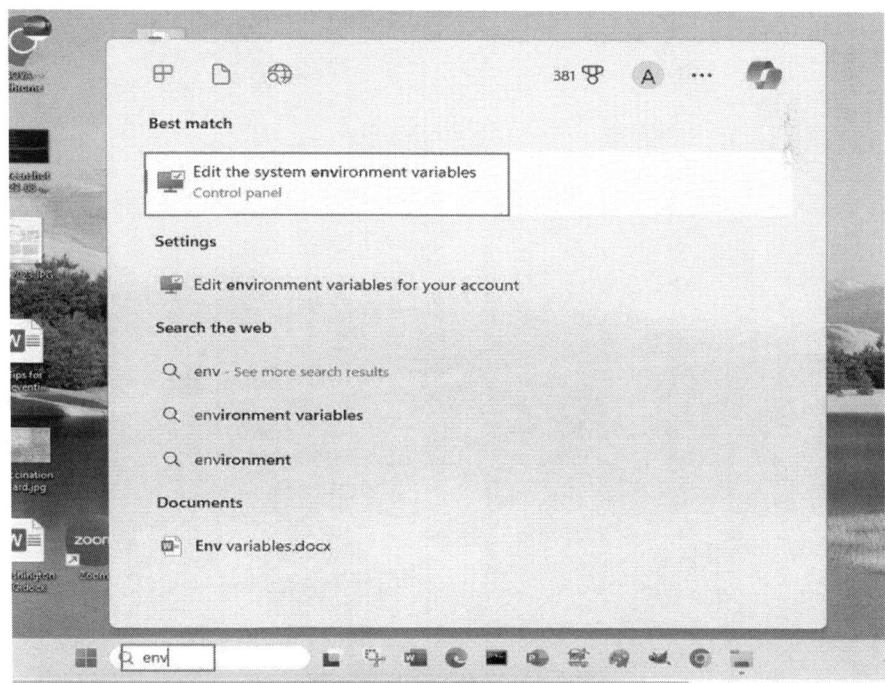

17

Environment Variables

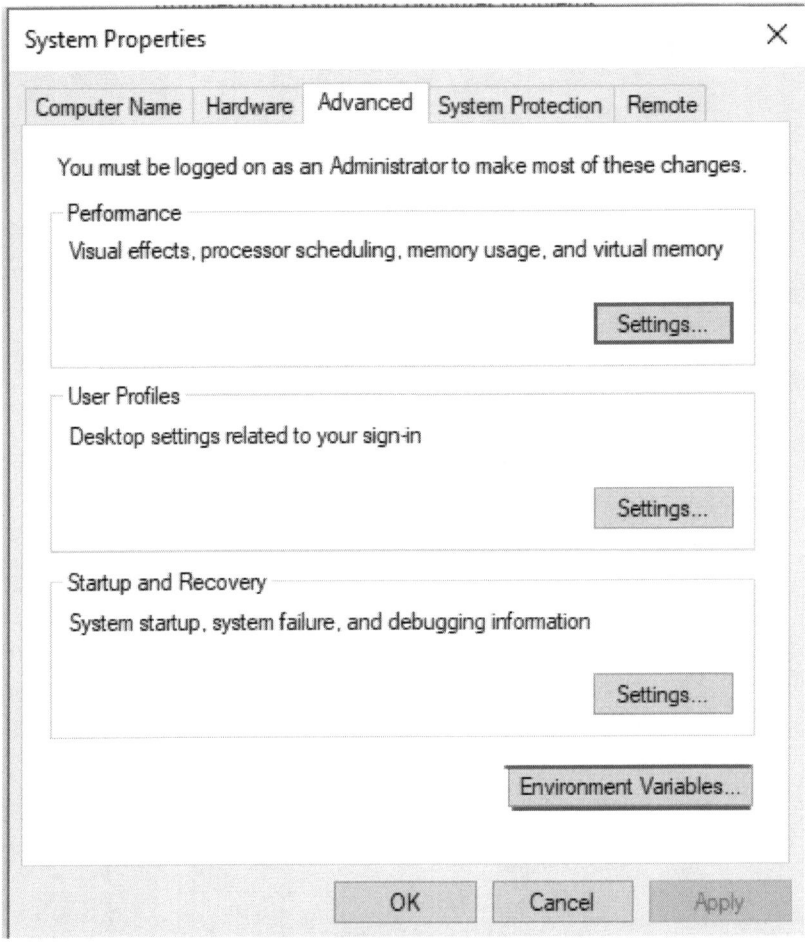

Add the JAVA_HOME

Create New folder in System Variable settings

Add the JAVA_HOME
variable and specify the folder path as value, where you unzipped the downloaded Java package.

Click on 'NEW'

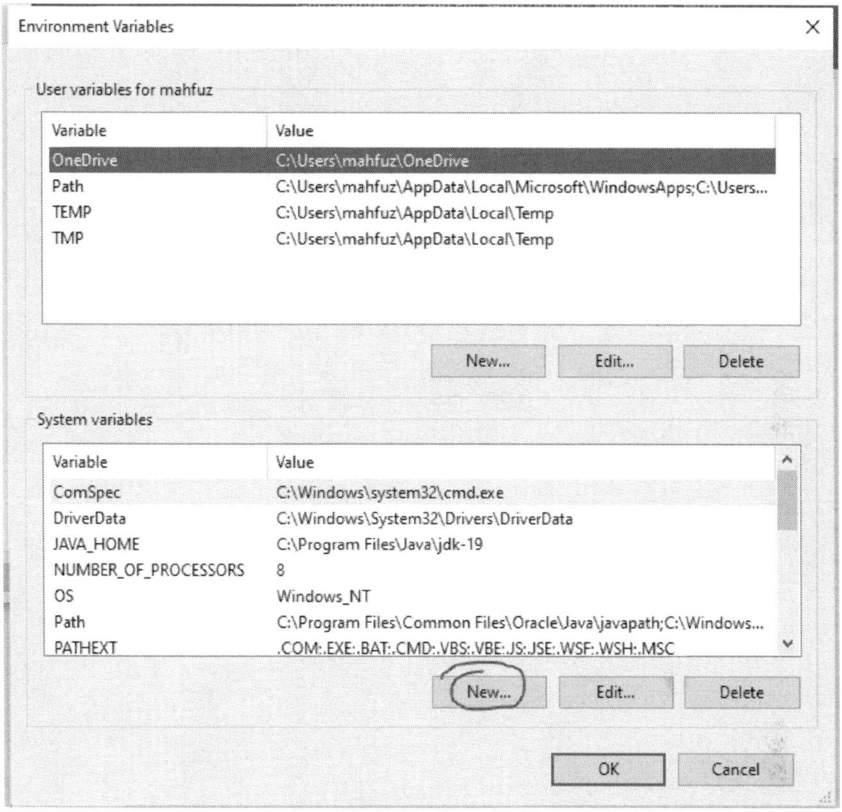

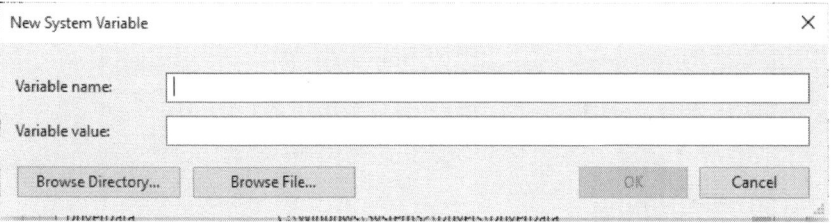

NEW SYSTEM VARIABLE MODULE POPS UP

Type Variable name-JAVA_HOME

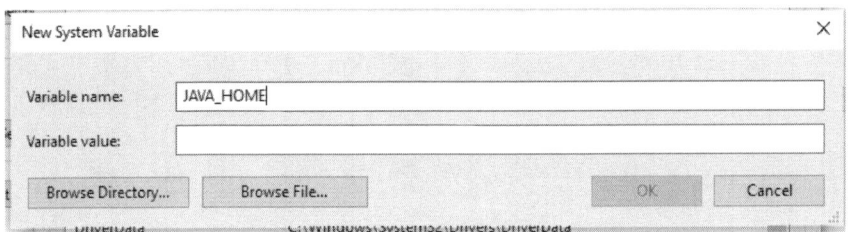

Go to the folder where Java located

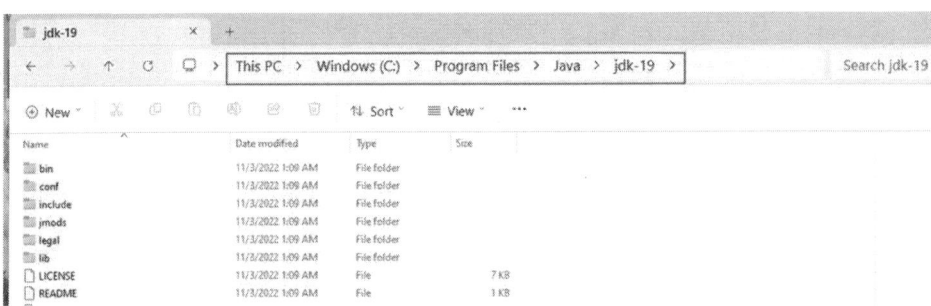

Copy the Path-Address
C:\Program Files\Java\jdk-19

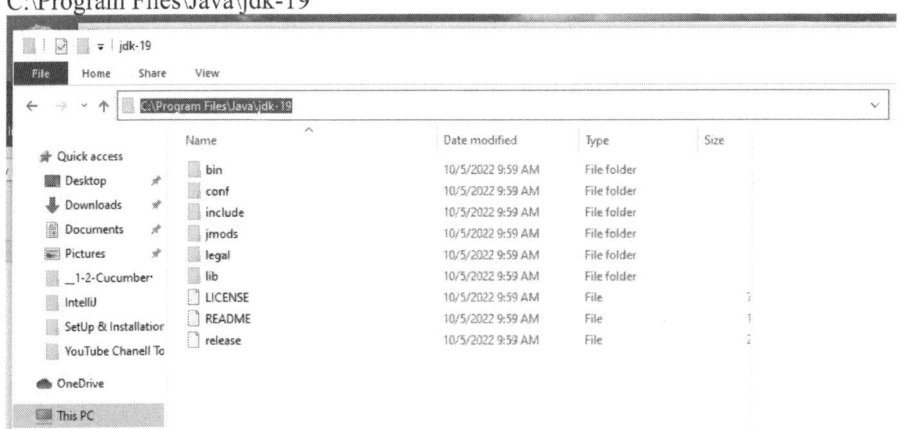

20

Paste the copied path

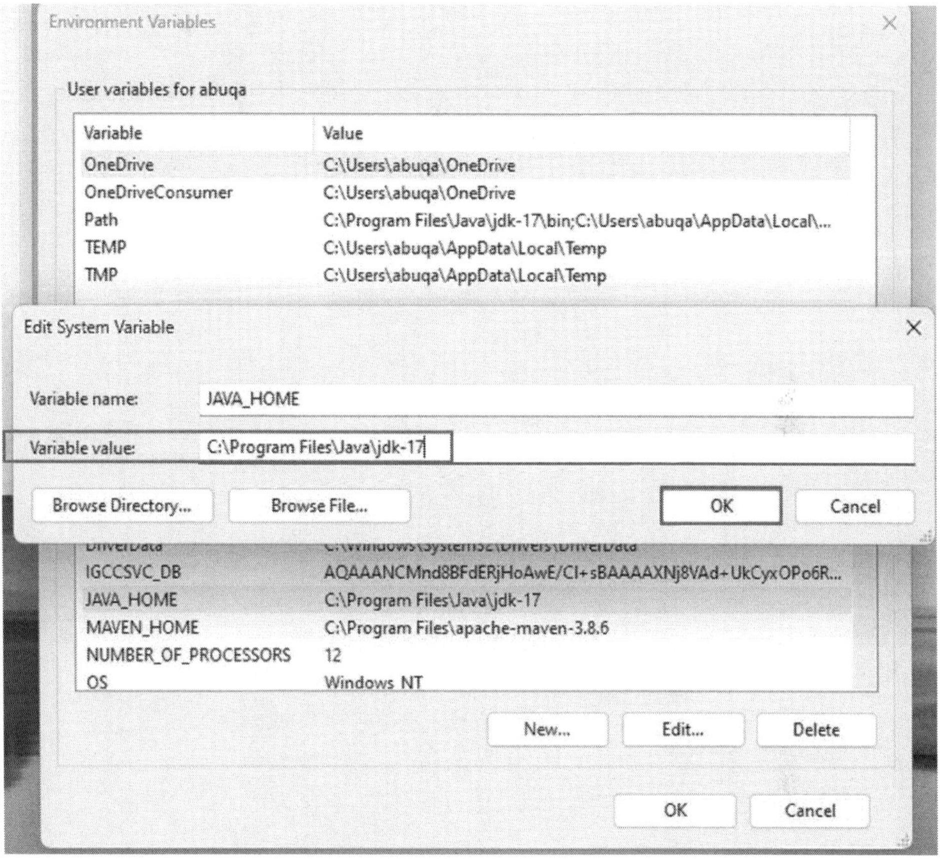

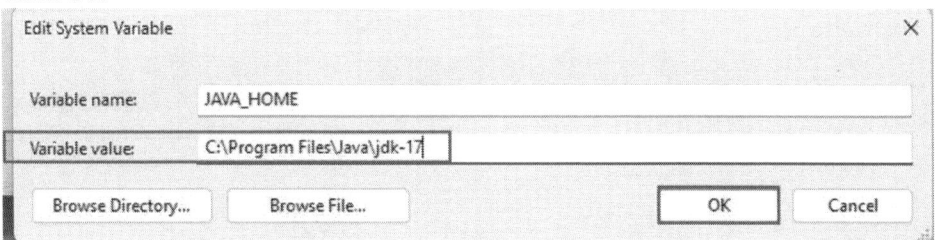

Click OK

Edit PATH -Env Variable

Select Path on Env. Variable Module then Click on Edit button

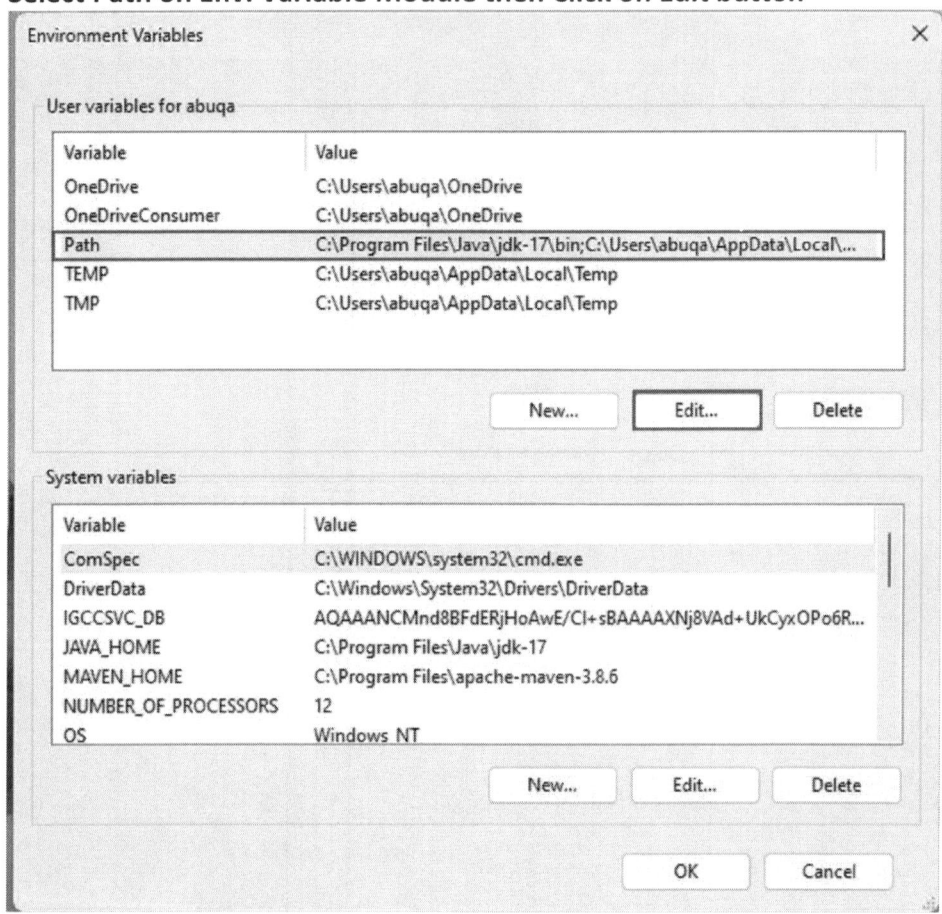

Update the PATH variable
Add a new path in the list which is the **bin** folder inside the JDK folder

Create new path Env variable Module

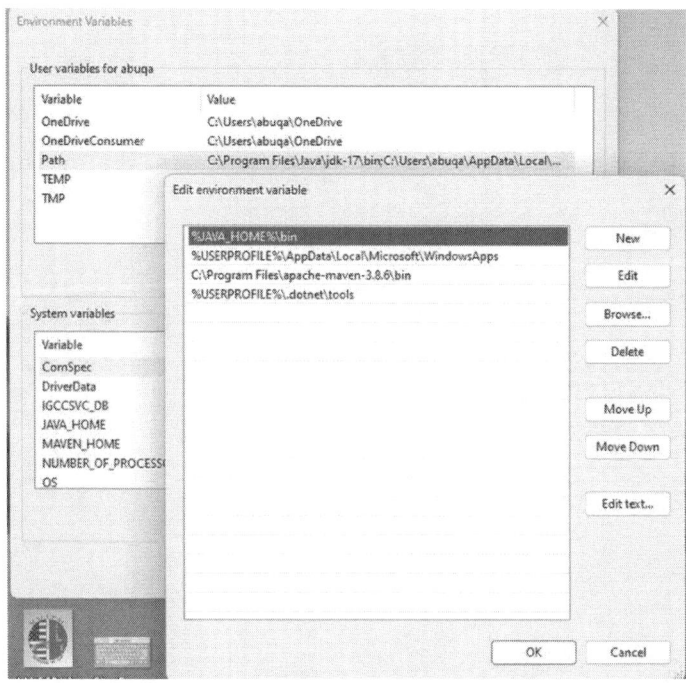

Crate a Click on New Button

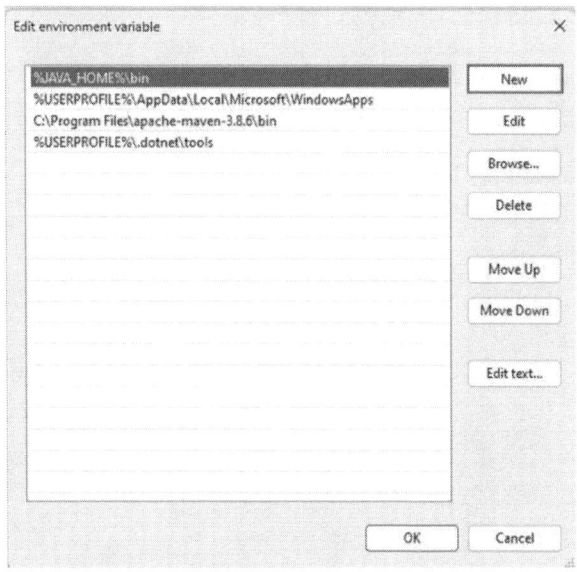

Paste the bin folder Path here

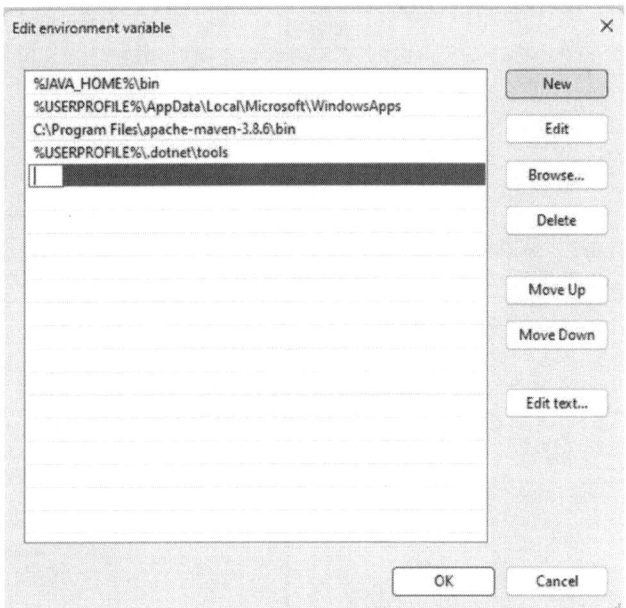

To find path Go to Bin folder in Java folder

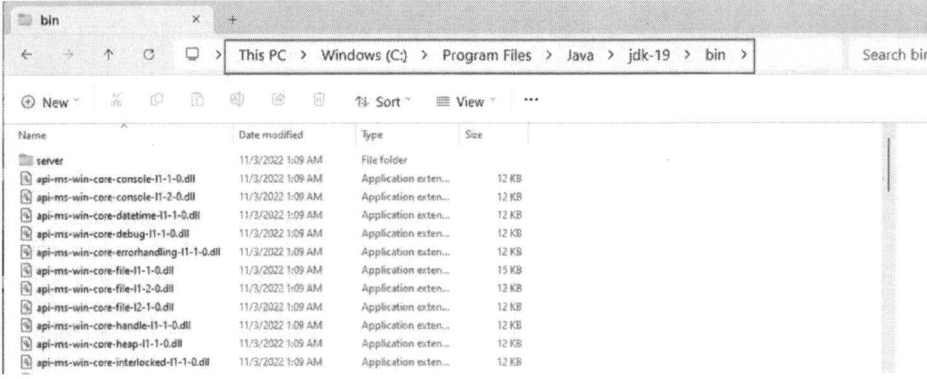

Copy the Bin folder path

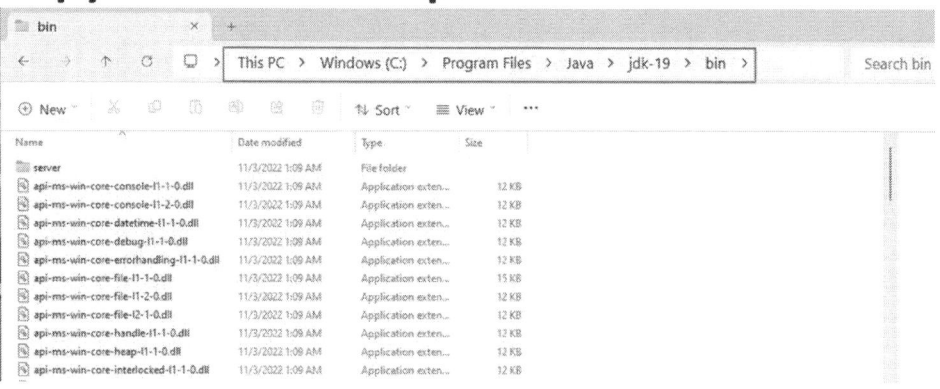

Paste java > bin address into the new line

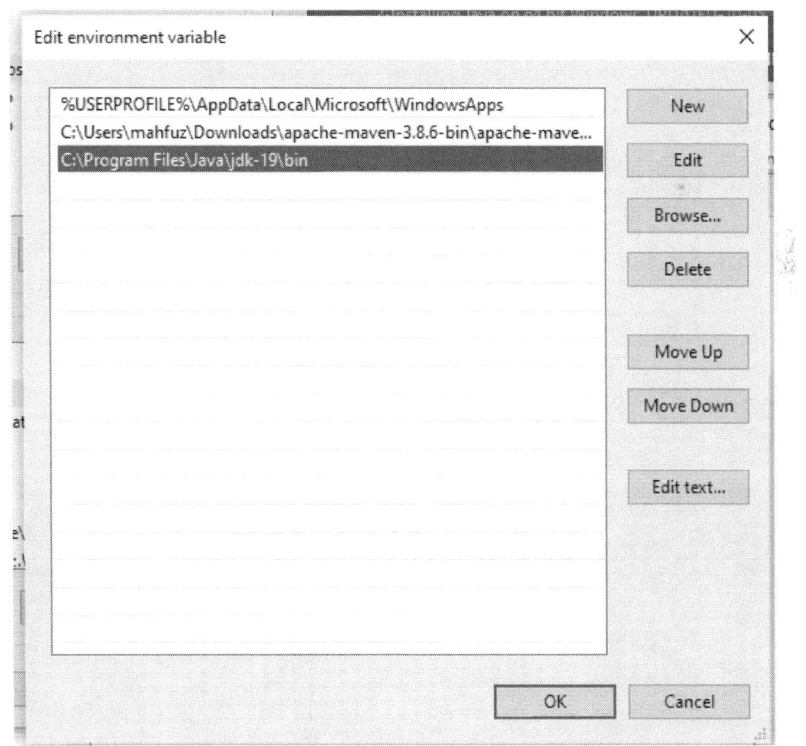

Click OK

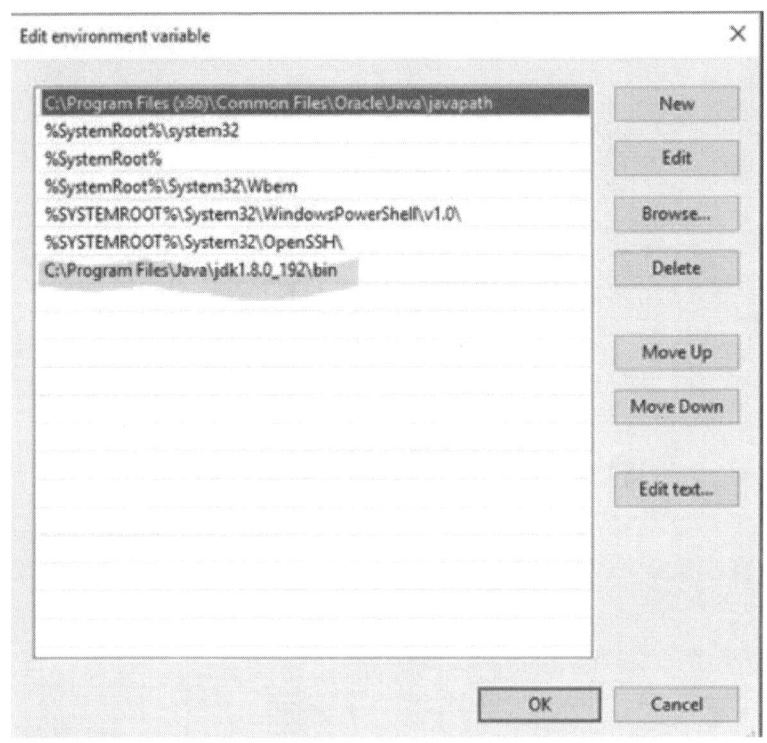

Now Check if Java Installed

Java --version

JAVA Recognized after env variable config

```
Command Prompt
Microsoft Windows [Version 10.0.19044.1288]
(c) Microsoft Corporation. All rights reserved.

C:\Users\mahfuz>java -version
java version "19" 2022-09-20
Java(TM) SE Runtime Environment (build 19+36-2238)
Java HotSpot(TM) 64-Bit Server VM (build 19+36-2238, mixed mode, sharing)

C:\Users\mahfuz>
```

Echo %JAVA_HOME%

```
C:\Users\mahfu>echo %JAVA_HOME%
C:\Program Files\Java\jdk-19

C:\Users\mahfu>
```

Verify Java Installation in Program

To verify that Java has been installed on your computer, open a new command prompt. Type the below command which will print the version of Java installed on your computer.

Verify Java & jdk inside Program file

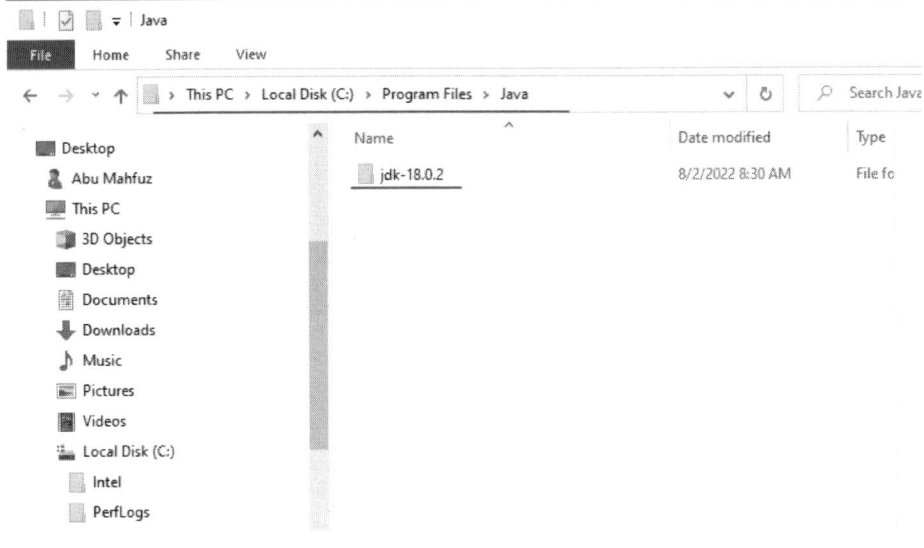

Install Eclipse IDE

Download & Install Eclipse

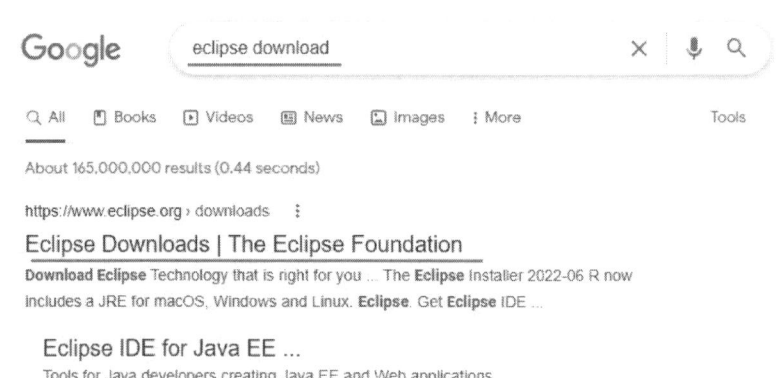

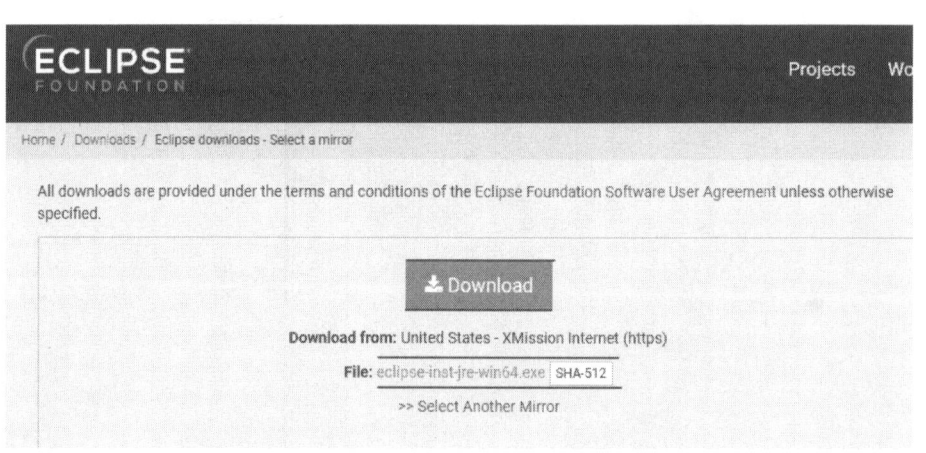

Download correct and latest version

The Eclipse Installer 2022-06 R now includes a JRE for macOS, Windows and Linux.

Get **Eclipse IDE 2022-06**

Install your favorite desktop IDE packages.

Download x86_64

Download Packages | Need Help?

Eclipse IDE for Java Developer

User Agreement

Remember Location Eclipse to Installed

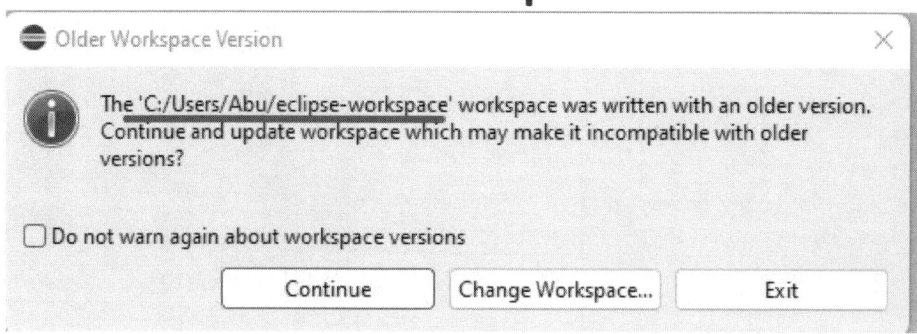

Start Java Project in Eclipse

Click on File > New > Java Project

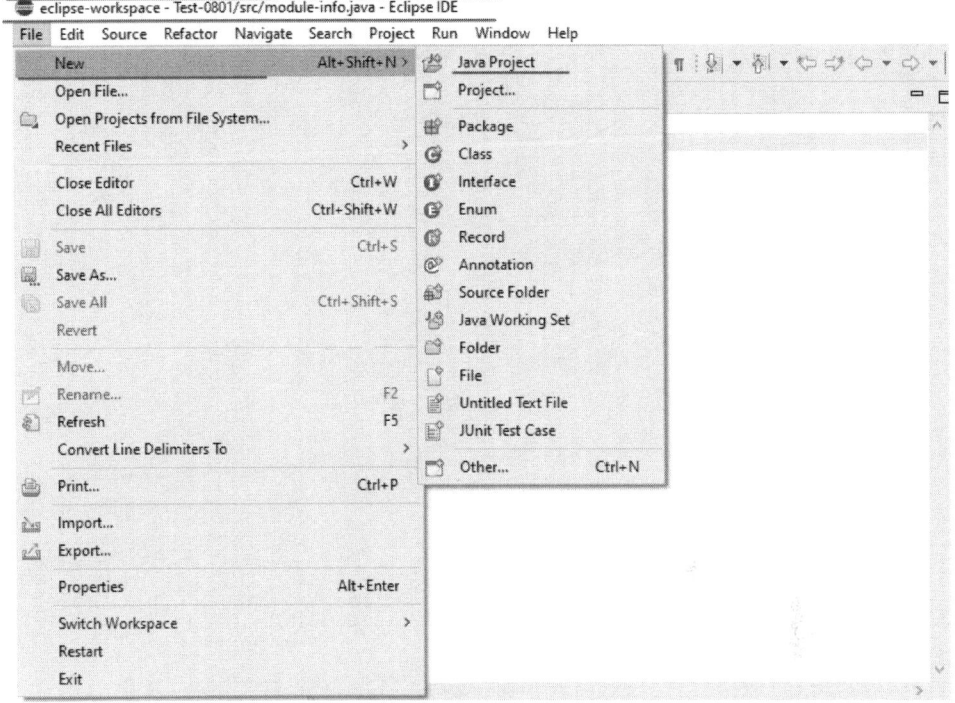

Give a Project Name

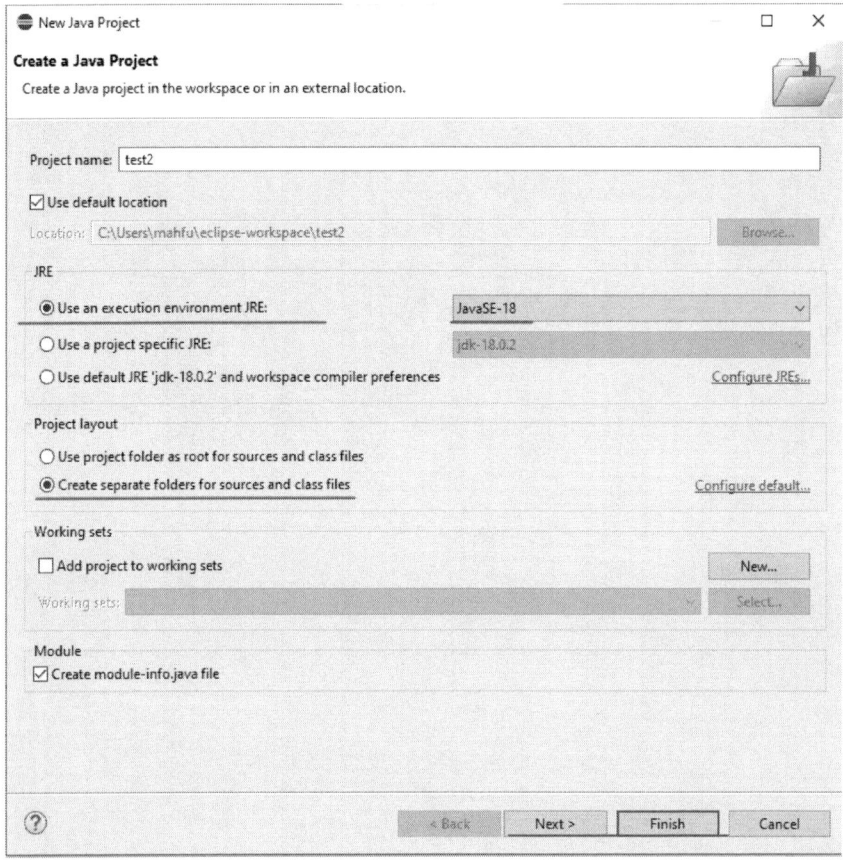

PROJECT VIEW IN ECLIPSE

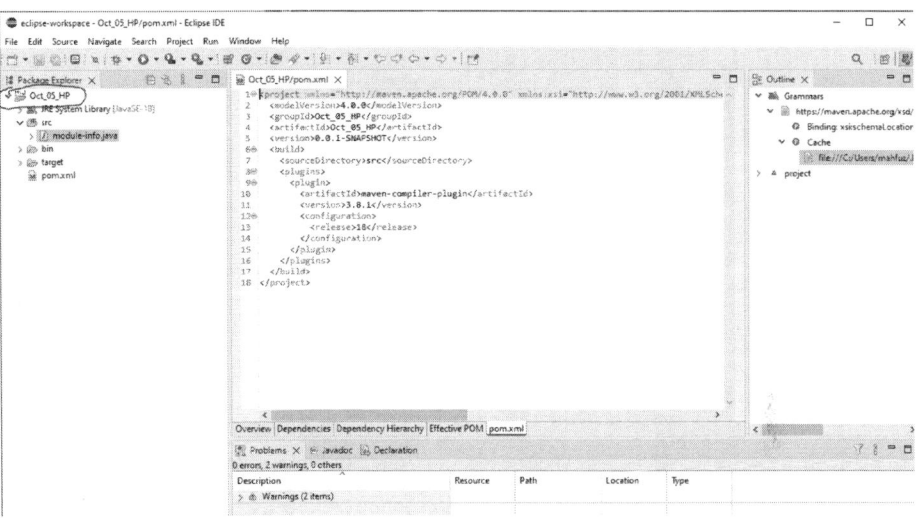

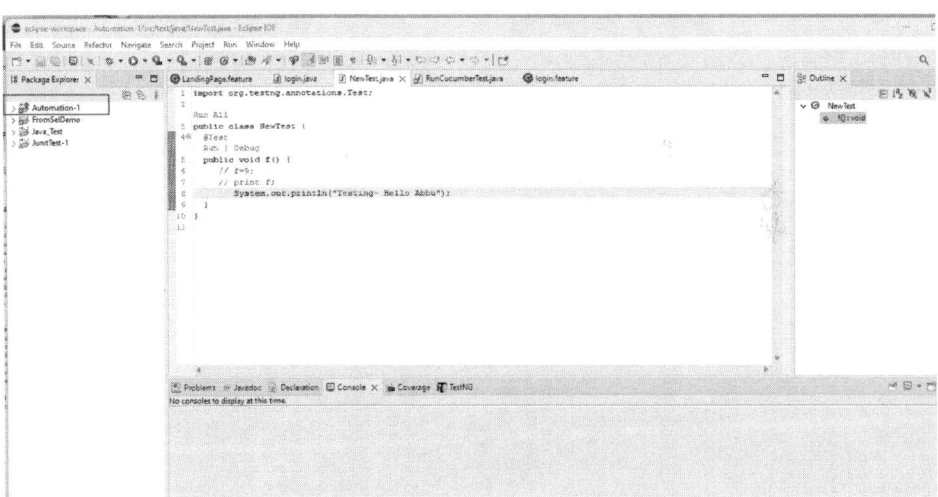

Update to latest version of Eclipse

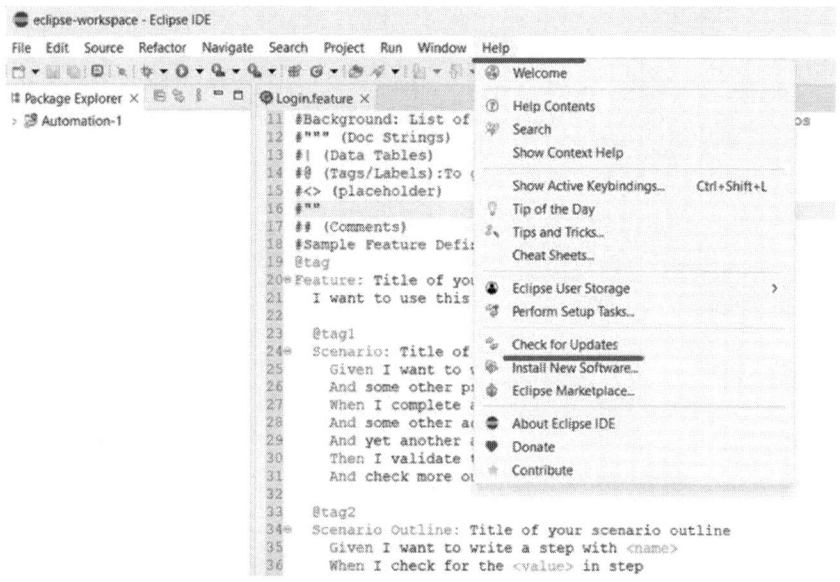

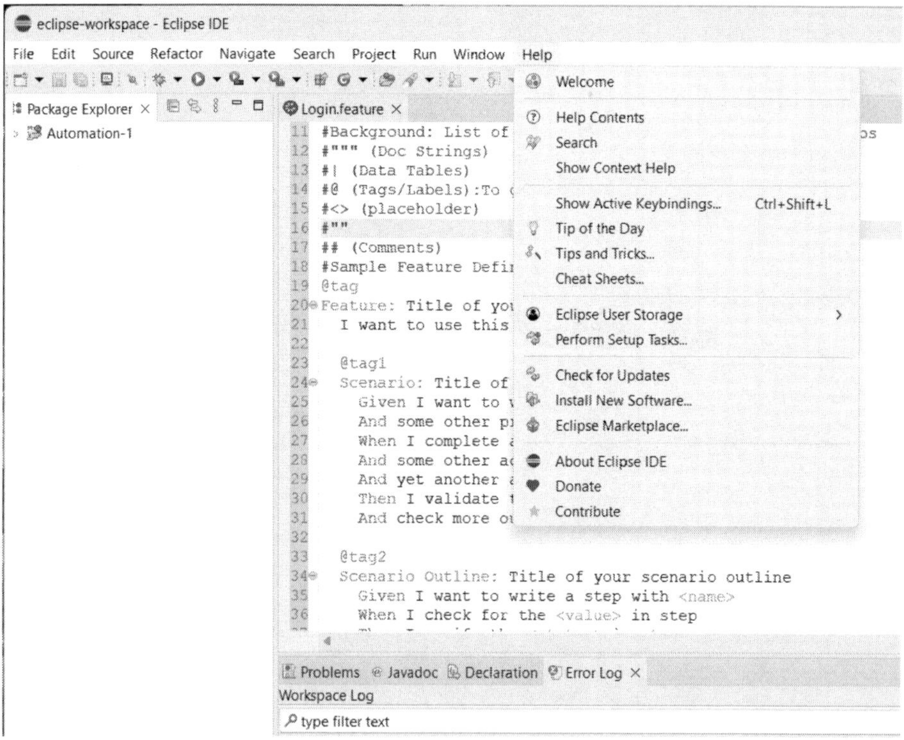

Apache Maven

DOWNLOAD MAVEN
Download the correct version bin – zip file

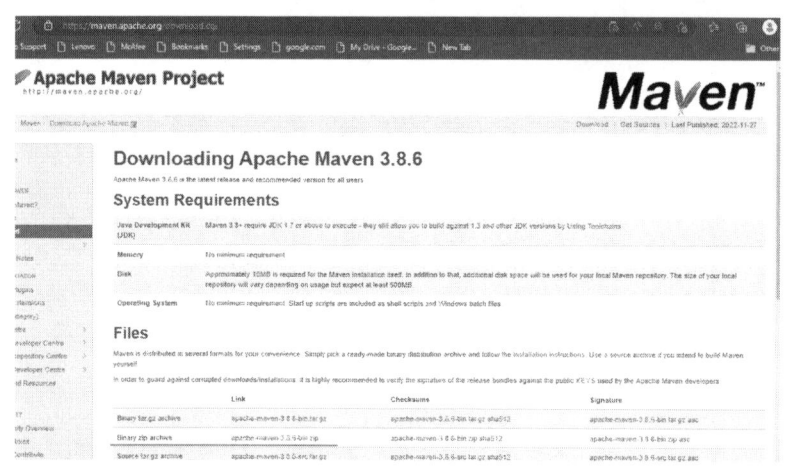

Unzip- extract the folder

Move or Copy Downloaded file from Download folder to
Program folder

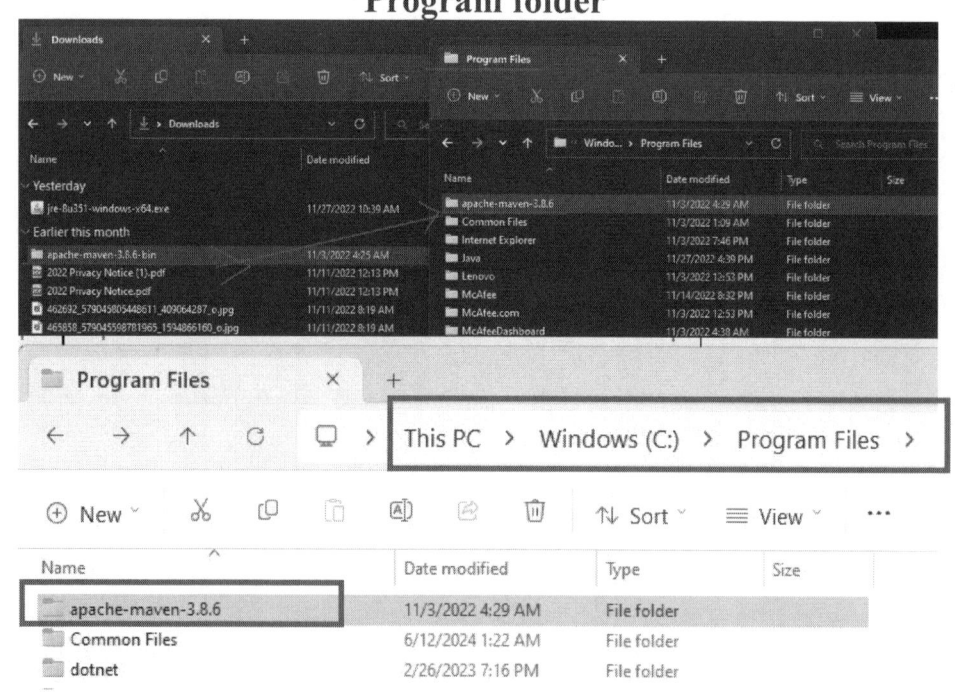

Maven Env Setup

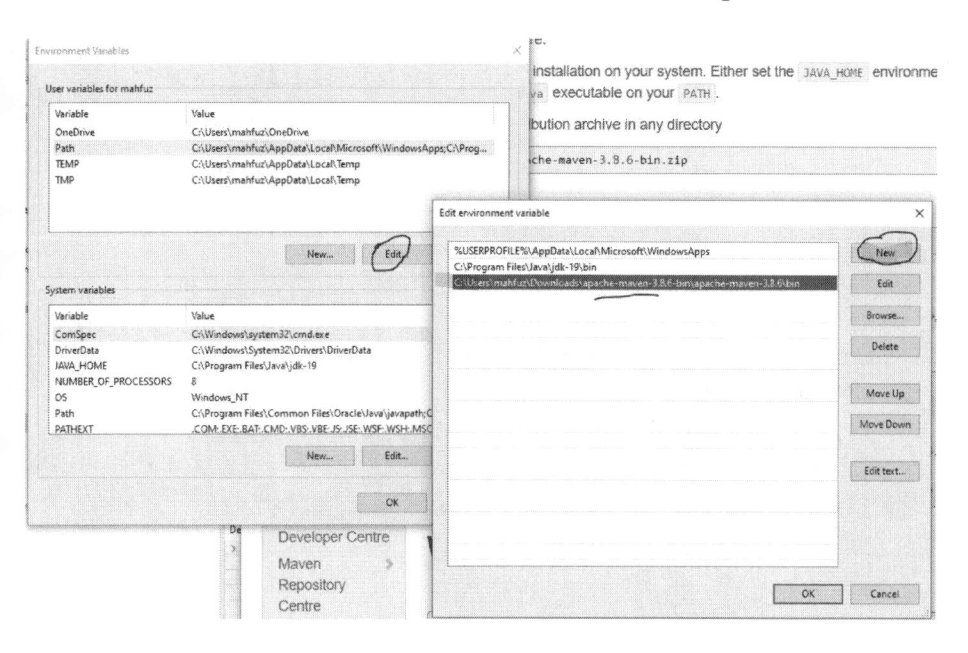

Locate 'Maven Home' in your computer

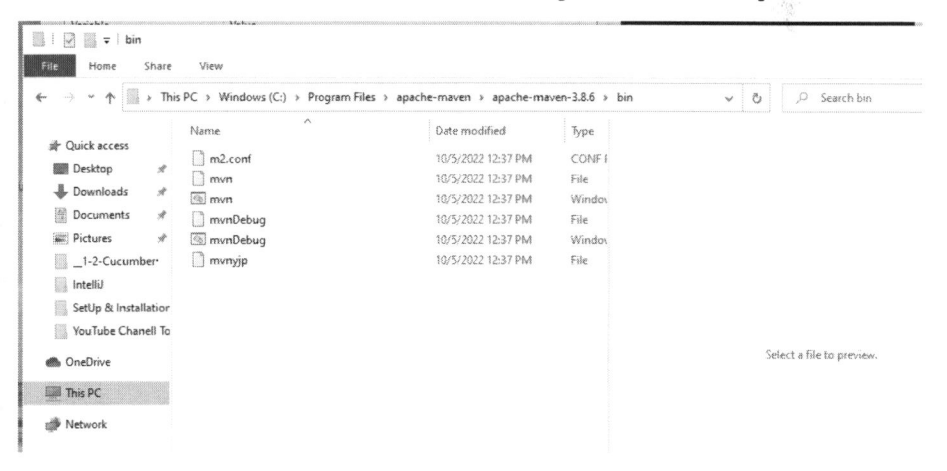

Copy the Address

C:\Program Files\apache-maven

Paste in the

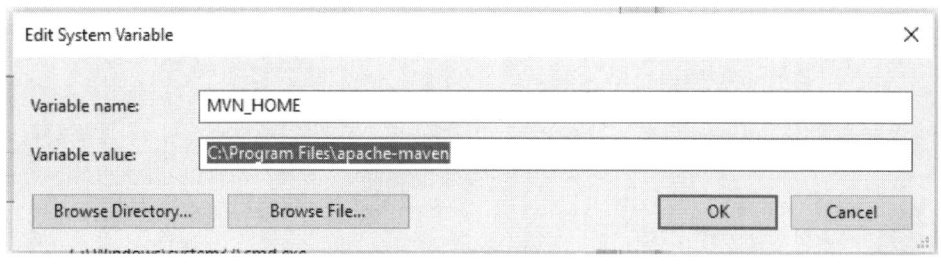

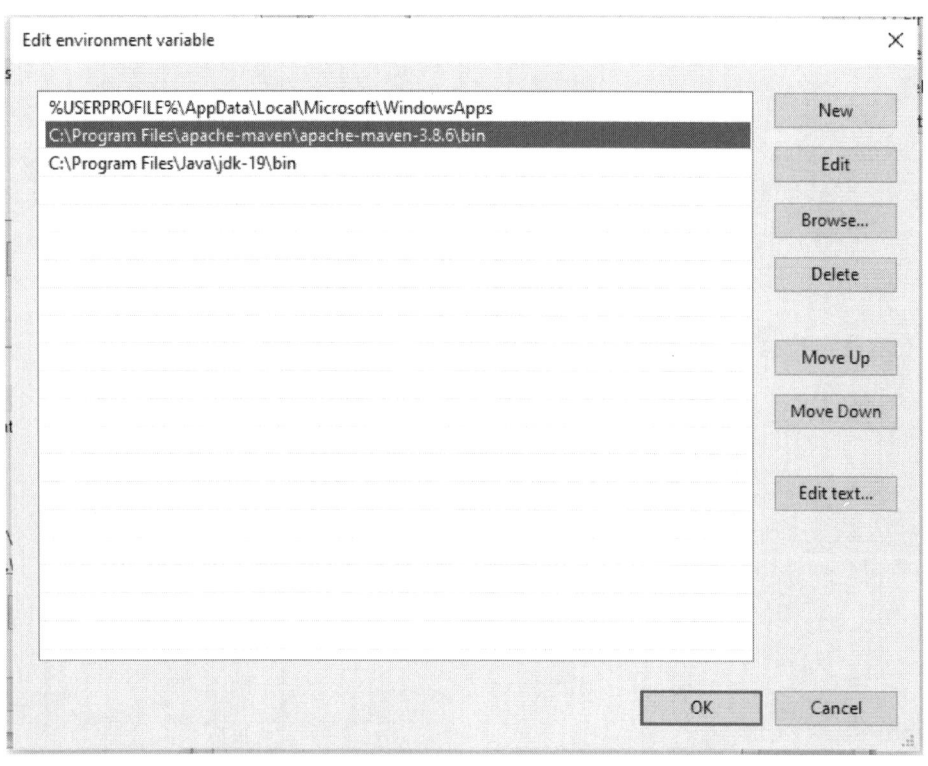

Edit Maven Path

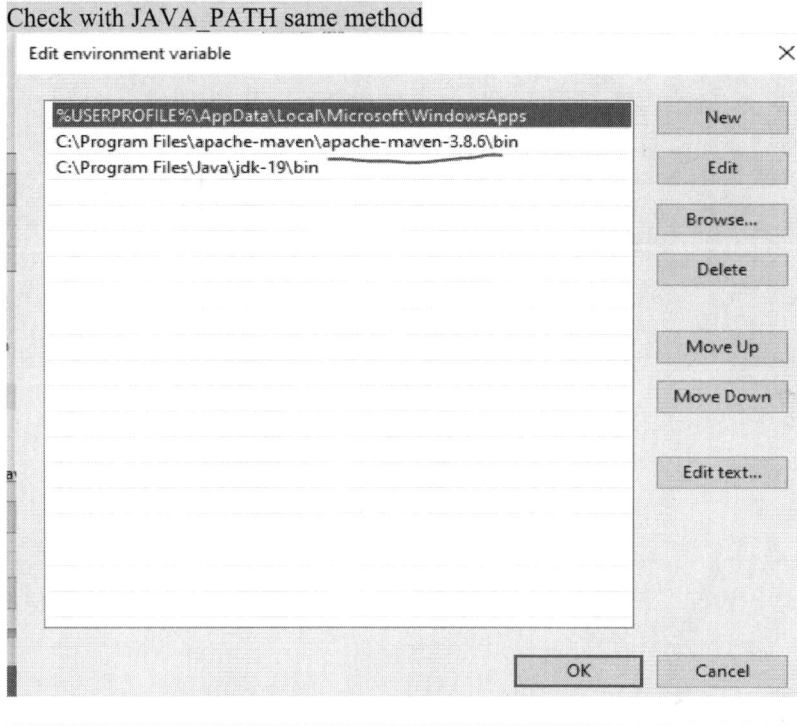

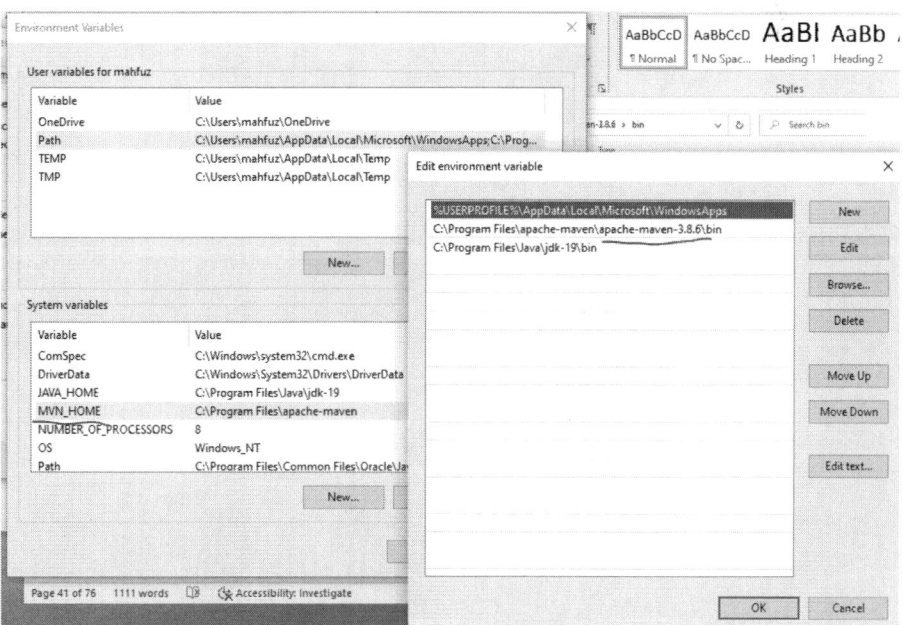

Check with JAVA_PATH same method

Check if Maven installation displays

```
Command Prompt

Microsoft Windows [Version 10.0.22631.3880]
(c) Microsoft Corporation. All rights reserved.

C:\Users\abuqa>mvn -v
Apache Maven 3.8.6 (84538c9988a25aec085021c365c560670ad80f63)
Maven home: C:\Program Files\apache-maven-3.8.6
Java version: 17.0.8, vendor: Oracle Corporation, runtime: C:\Program Files\Java\jdk-17
Default locale: en_US, platform encoding: Cp1252
OS name: "windows 11", version: "10.0", arch: "amd64", family: "windows"

C:\Users\abuqa>
```

Name	Date modified	Type	Size
apache-maven-3.8.6	11/3/2022 4:29 AM	File folder	
Common Files	6/12/2024 1:22 AM	File folder	
dotnet	2/26/2023 7:16 PM	File folder	
Flip PDF Plus Pro	4/26/2023 9:11 AM	File folder	
GIMP 2	6/23/2023 11:21 AM	File folder	
Git	1/31/2023 11:07 PM	File folder	
Google	4/26/2023 10:34 AM	File folder	
HP	4/28/2023 11:08 AM	File folder	
HPPrintScanDoctor	6/22/2024 3:38 AM	File folder	
Inknoe ClassPoint 2	11/23/2023 9:34 PM	File folder	
Internet Explorer	6/12/2024 1:22 AM	File folder	
Java	8/30/2023 3:23 PM	File folder	

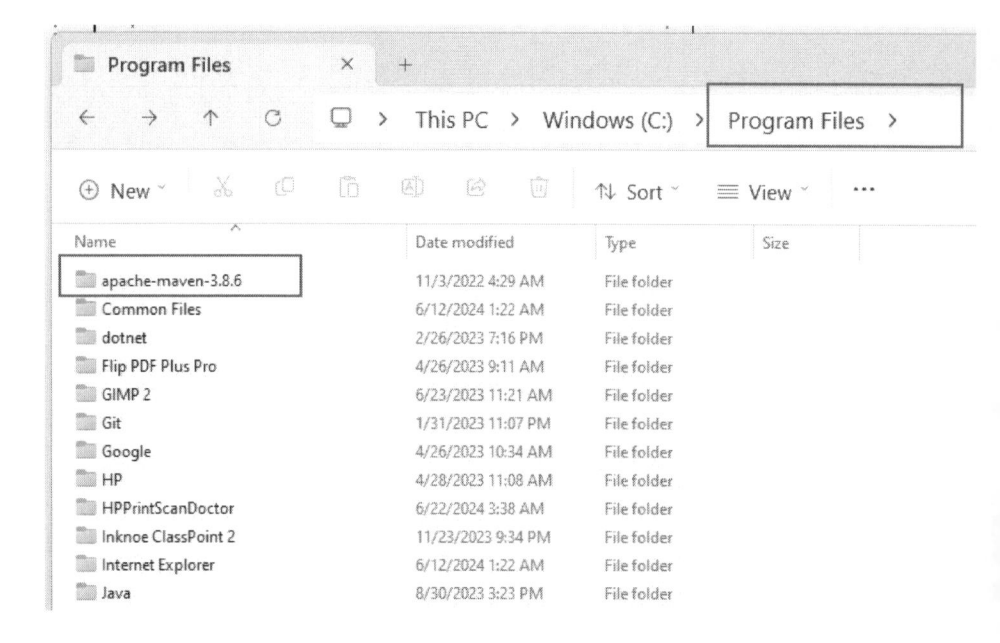

Start a Maven Project

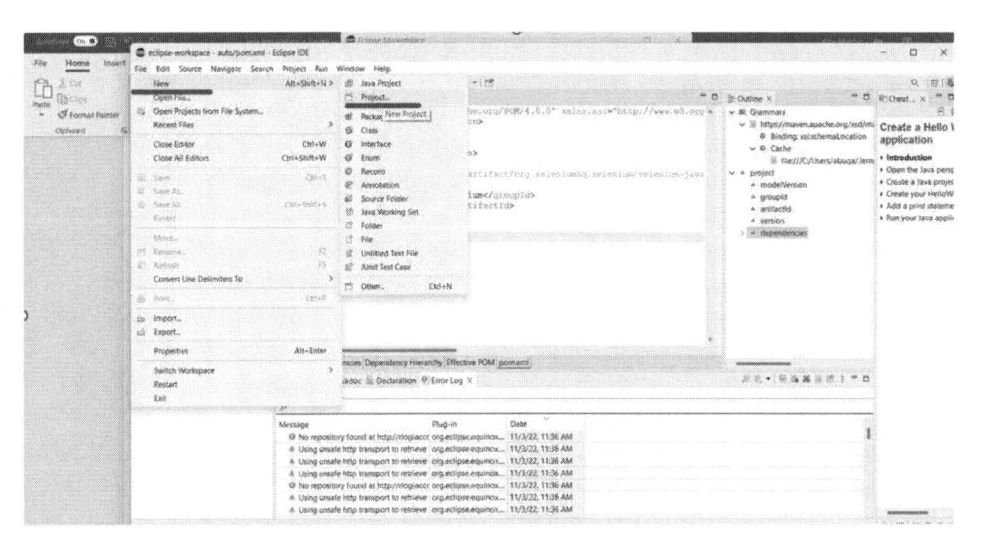

Select the Maven Project

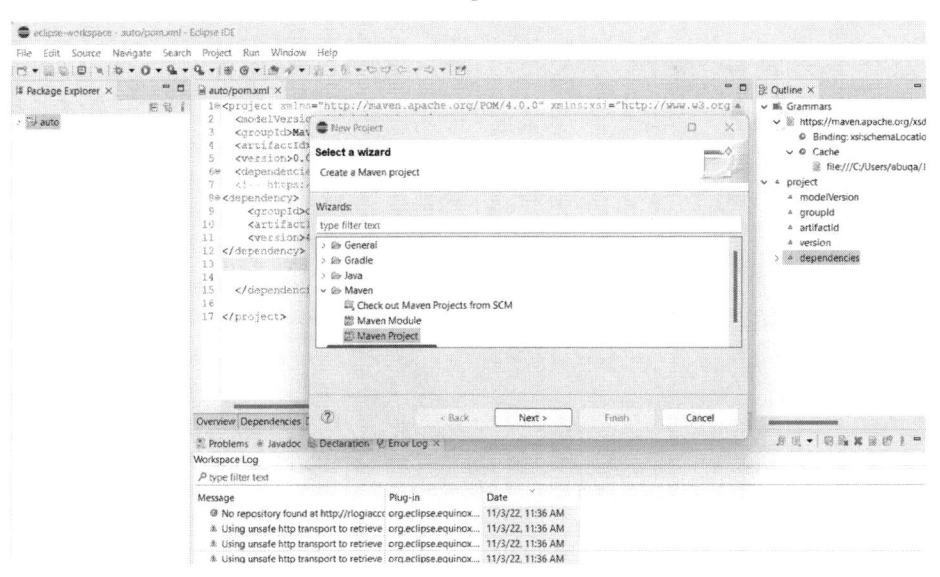

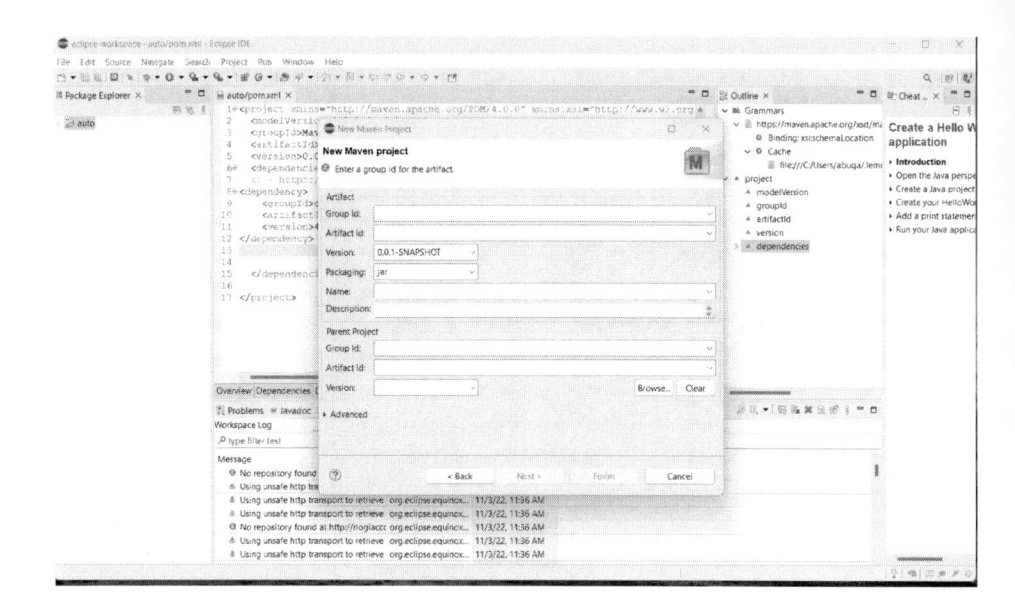

Convert Java Project to Maven Project

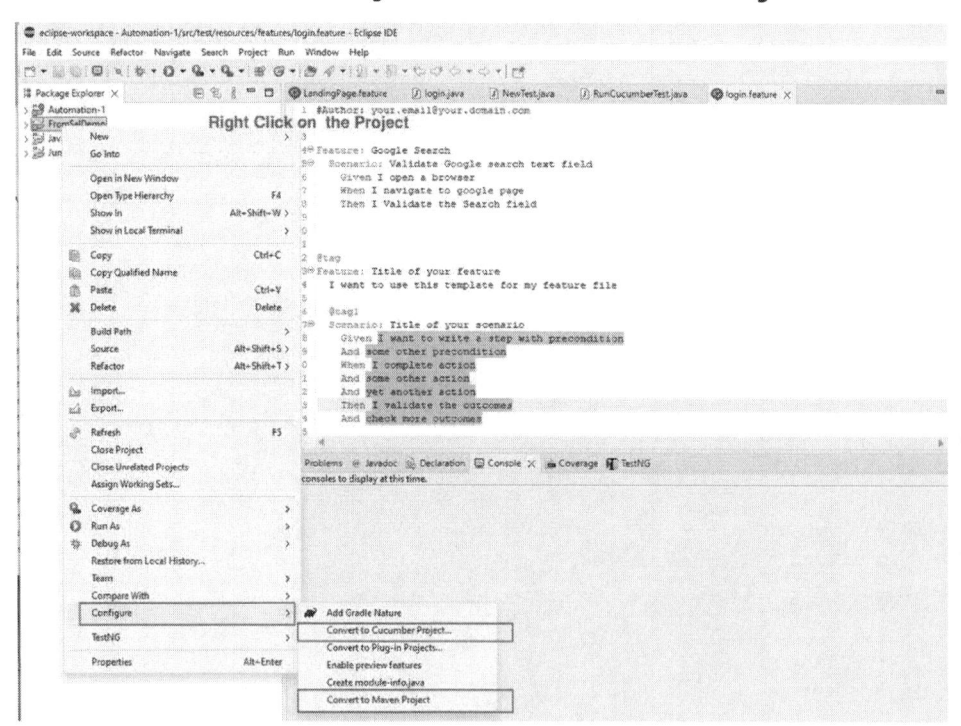

44

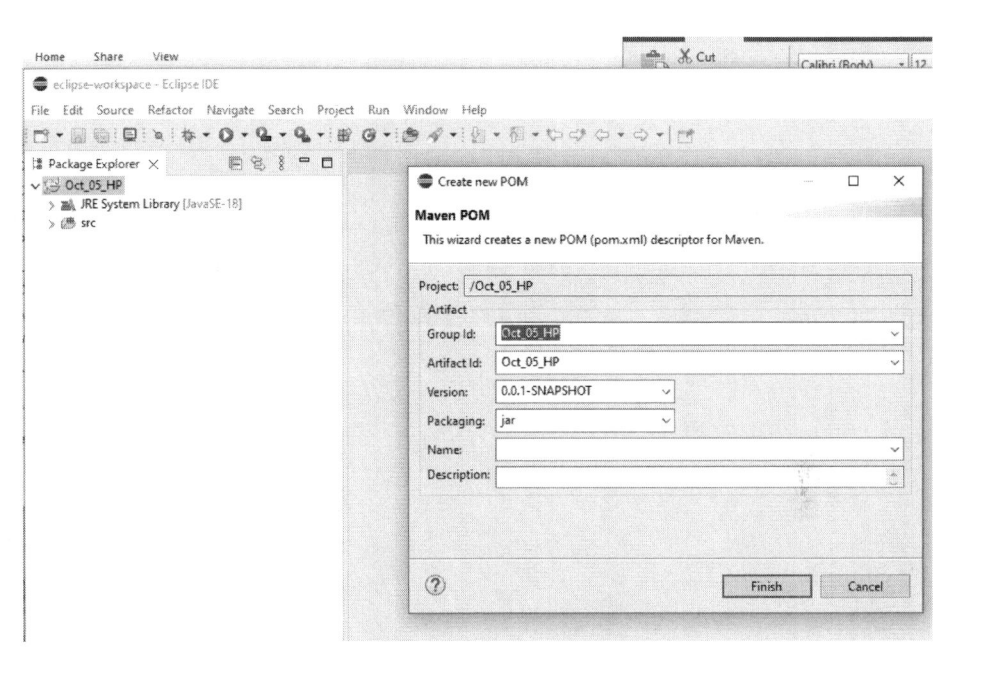

POM.XML file added to the project

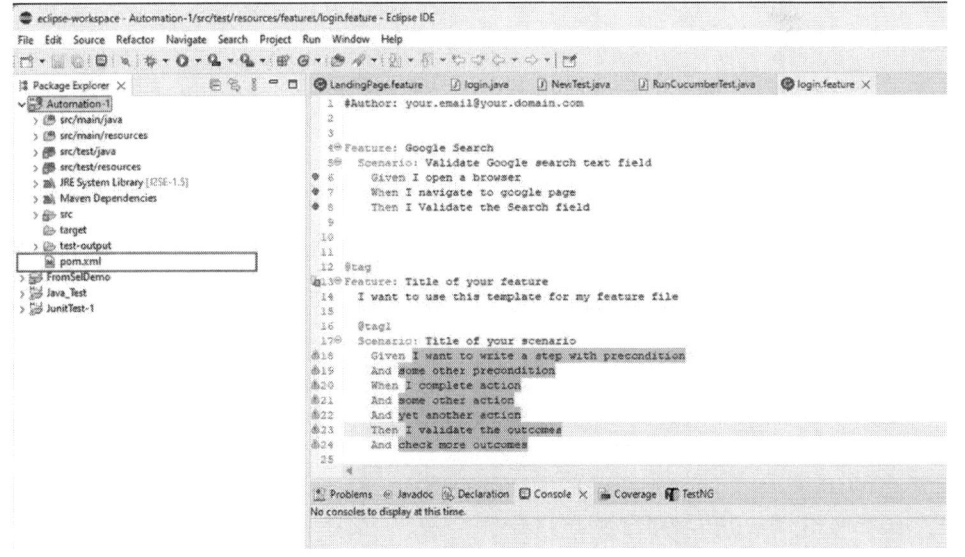

45

Selenium

Selenium with different version/options

Ruby
C#
Java
Python
JavaScirpt

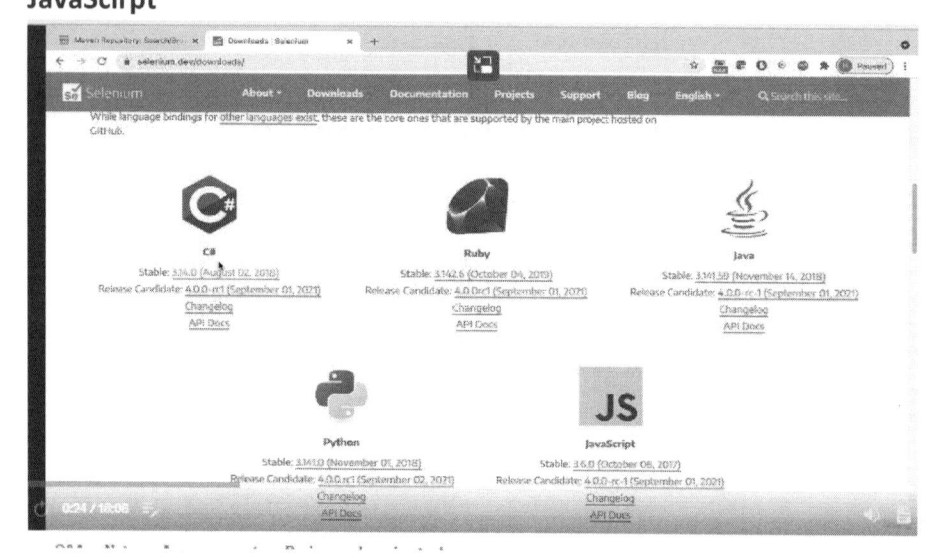

Add Selenium-Java

Select the latest stable version

SELENIUM DEPENDENCY FILE

Add Dependency file to Dependencies in Pom.xml file

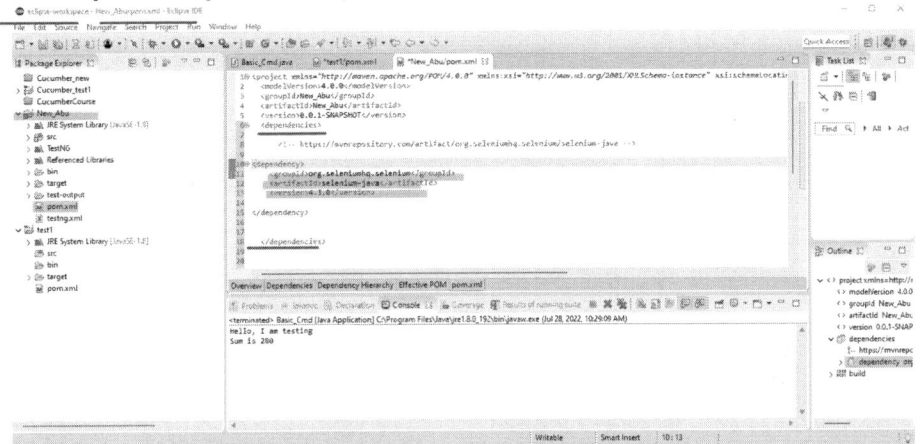

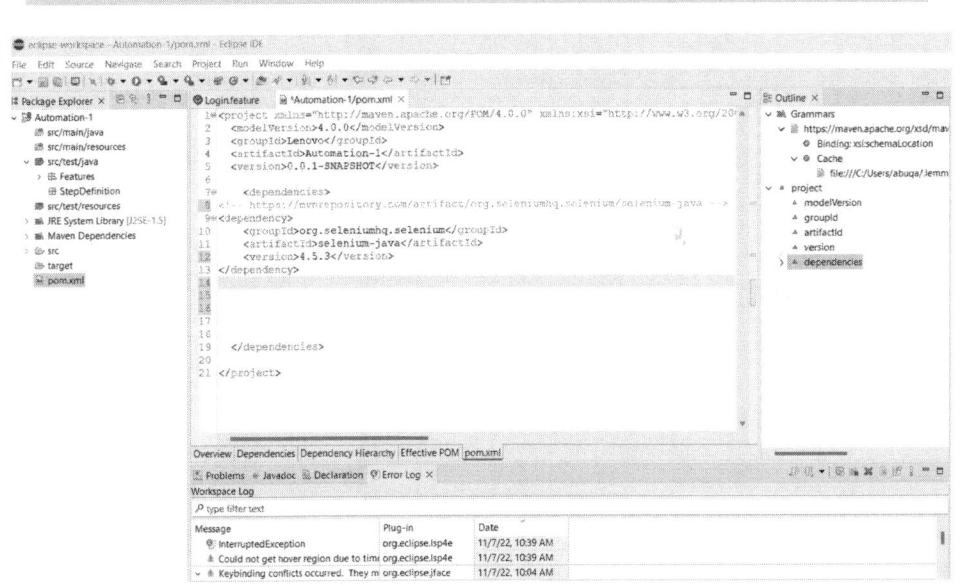

Copy selenium Dependency

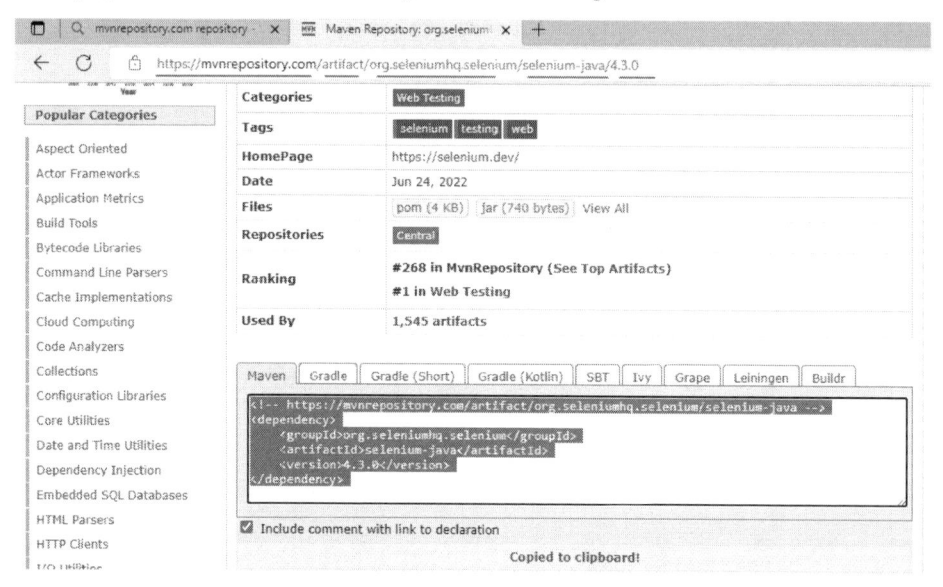

Paste Dependency added in to POM file

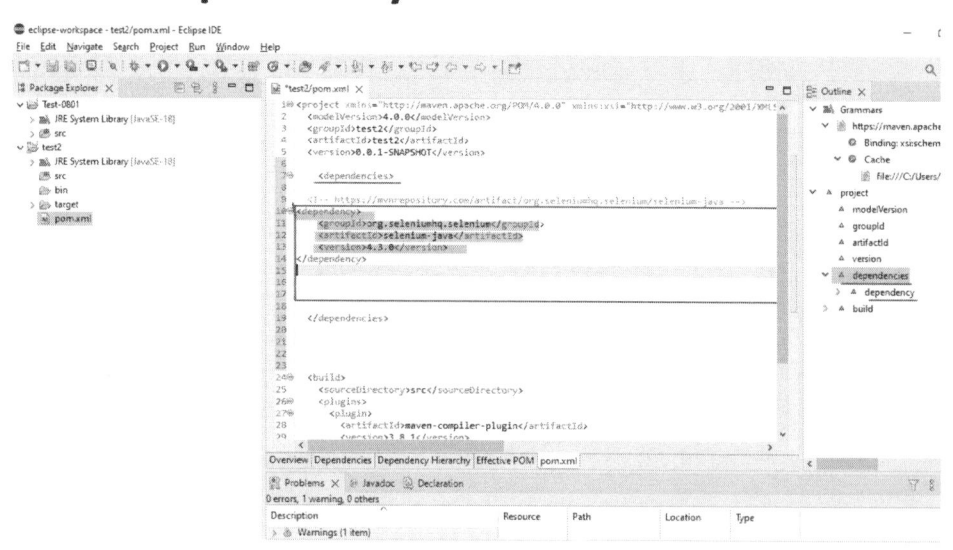

TestNG

TestNG Installation & Setup

Go to mvnrepository.com and search for TestNG

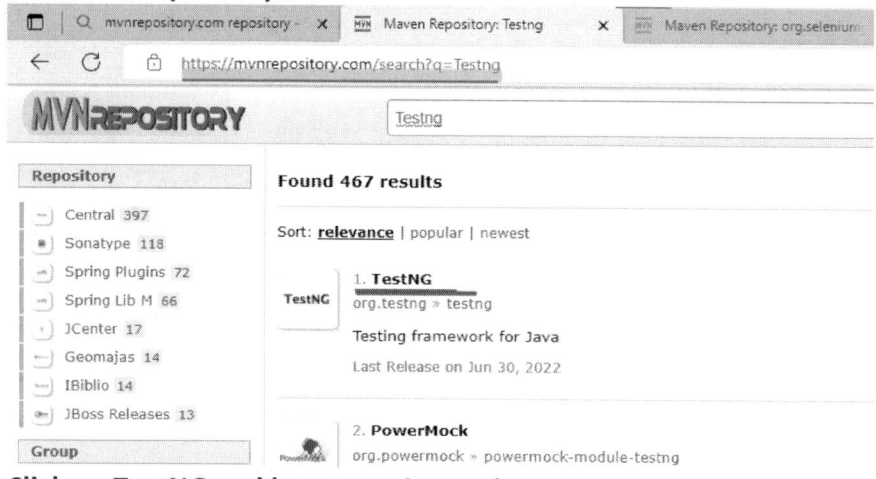

Click on TestNG and latest version and

copy the code

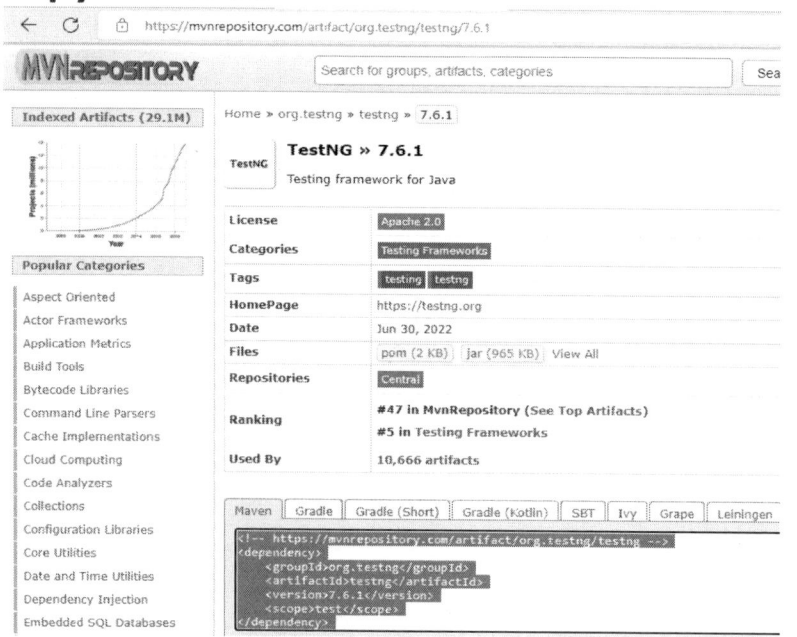

52

Paste in to your Project POM.xml file

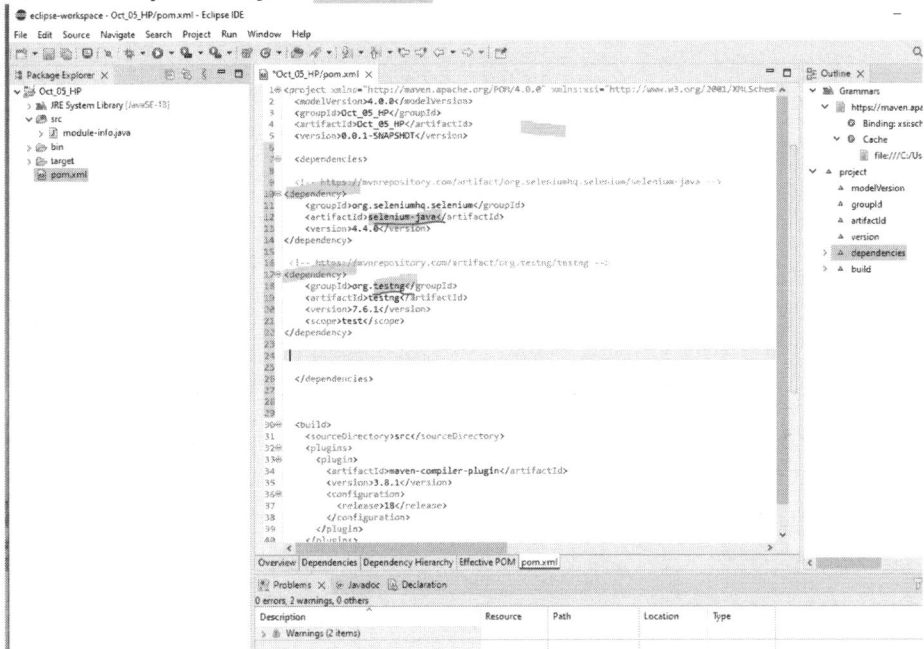

Added Selenium & TestNG Dependencies:

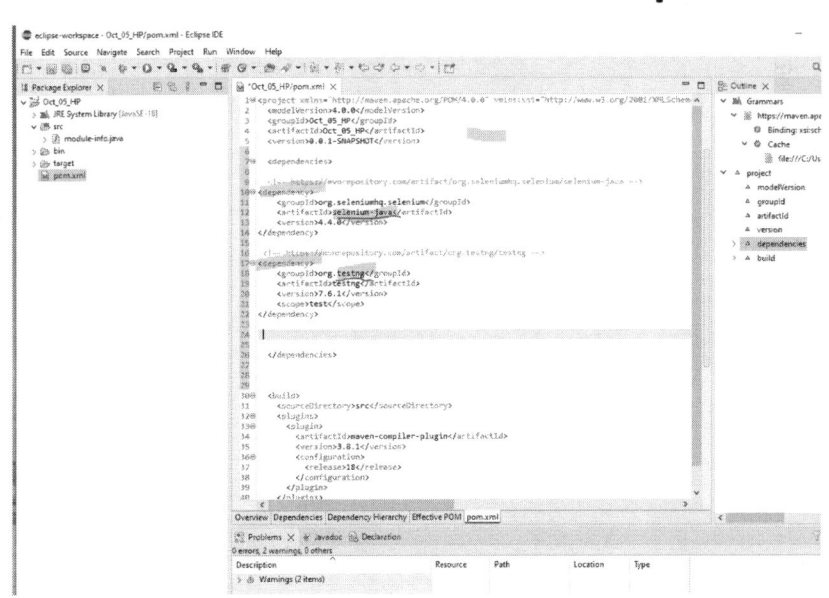

Junit

JUnit Installation and Setup

Sample Dependencies

Cucumber
```xml
<dependencies>
<!-- https://mvnrepository.com/artifact/org.seleniumhq.selenium/selenium-java -->
<dependency>
    <groupId>org.seleniumhq.selenium</groupId>
    <artifactId>selenium-java</artifactId>
    <version>4.5.3</version>
</dependency>


<!-- https://mvnrepository.com/artifact/io.cucumber/cucumber-java -->
<dependency>
    <groupId>io.cucumber</groupId>
    <artifactId>cucumber-java</artifactId>
    <version>7.9.0</version>
</dependency>

  <!-- https://mvnrepository.com/artifact/junit/junit -->
<dependency>
    <groupId>junit</groupId>
    <artifactId>junit</artifactId>
    <version>4.13.2</version>
    <scope>test</scope>
</dependency>


  <!-- https://mvnrepository.com/artifact/io.cucumber/cucumber-junit -->
<dependency>
    <groupId>io.cucumber</groupId>
    <artifactId>cucumber-junit</artifactId>
    <version>2.0.0</version>
    <scope>test</scope>
</dependency>



  <!-- https://mvnrepository.com/artifact/org.testng/testng -->
<dependency>
    <groupId>org.testng</groupId>
    <artifactId>testng</artifactId>
    <version>7.6.1</version>
    <scope>test</scope>
</dependency>
```

```xml
<!-- https://mvnrepository.com/artifact/io.cucumber/cucumber-testng -->
<dependency>
    <groupId>io.cucumber</groupId>
    <artifactId>cucumber-testng</artifactId>
    <version>7.8.0</version>
</dependency>


  </dependencies>
```

Dependency file added to Eclipse after the file id was added to pom.xml file. For reference Udemy file

Made in the USA
Columbia, SC
28 July 2024